E S T A T E   P U B L I ...

ISLAND TOWNS

NEWPORT · RYDE · COWES · SANDO
YARMOUTH · TOTLAND · FRESHWA
BEMBRIDGE · BRADING · NITON

... RIDGE
...LL · SEAVIEW

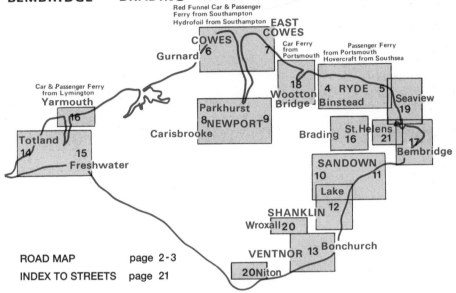

Red Funnel Car & Passenger Ferry from Southampton
Hydrofoil from Southampton

EAST COWES

COWES 6 7

Gurnard

Car Ferry from Portsmouth

Passenger Ferry from Portsmouth
Hovercraft from Southsea

Car & Passenger Ferry from Lymington
Yarmouth

18
Wootton Bridge · Binstead

4 RYDE 5

Seaview 19

16

Parkhurst

8 NEWPORT 9

Carisbrooke

Brading St.Helens 16 21 17

Bembridge

Totland 14

15

Freshwater

SANDOWN 10 11

Lake

SHANKLIN 12

Wroxall 20

VENTNOR 13 Bonchurch

20 Niton

ROAD MAP   page 2-3

INDEX TO STREETS   page 21

Every effort has been made to verify the accuracy of information in this book but the publishers cannot accept responsibility for expense or loss caused by any error or omission. Information that will be of assistance to the user of the maps will be welcomed.

The representation of a road, track or footpath on the maps in this atlas is no evidence of the existence of a right of way.

One-way Street   →
Car Park   🅿
Place of Worship   ✚
Post Office   ●
Public Convenience   Ⓒ
Pedestrianized   ▨▨▨

Scale of street plans 4 inches to 1 mile
Unless otherwise stated

Street plans prepared and published by ESTATE PUBLICATIONS, Bridewell House, TENTERDEN, KENT, and based upon the ORDNANCE SURVEY maps with the sanction of the Controller of H. M. Stationery Office.

The publishers acknowledge the co-operation of The Isle of Wight Council in the preparation of these maps.

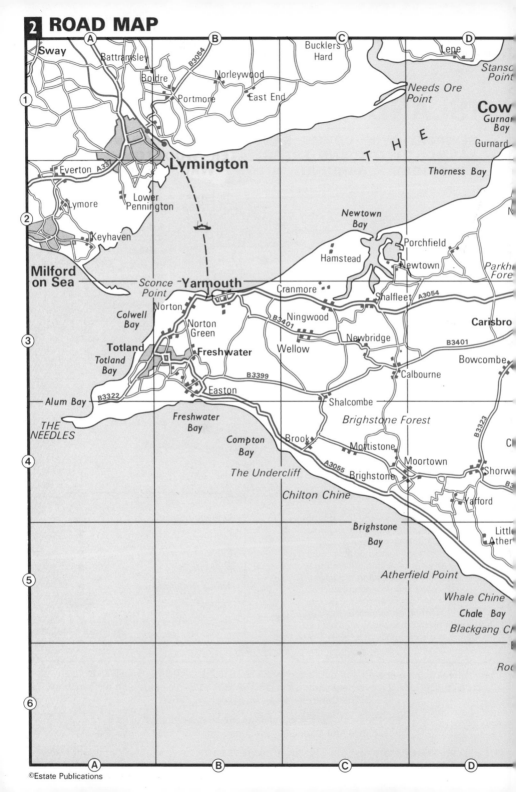

2 ROAD MAP

Sway
Battramsley
Boldre
Portmore
B3054
Norleywood
East End
Bucklers
Hard
Lepe
Stanso
Point

Needs Ore
Point

Cow

THE

Gurnar
Bay

Gurnard

Everton A337
Lymore
Lower
Pennington
Keyhaven

LYMINGTON

Thorness Bay

Newtown
Bay

Hamstead

Porchfield
Newtown

Parkh
Fore

N

Milford
on Sea
Sconce
Point
Yarmouth
Norton
Colwell
Bay
Norton
Green
Cranmore
Ningwood
B3401
Wellow
Newbridge
Shalfleet
A3054

Carisbro

B3401

Totland
Totland
Bay
Freshwater
Calbourne
Bowcombe

Alum Bay
B3322
B3399
Easton

Shalcombe

Brighstone Forest

B3323

THE
NEEDLES

Freshwater
Bay
Compton
Bay
The Undercliff
Brook
Mottistone
Moortown
Shorw
C
A3055
Brighstone

Chilton Chine

Yafford

Brighstone
Bay

Littl
Ather

Atherfield Point

Whale Chine
Chale Bay
Blackgang Cl

Roc

©Estate Publications

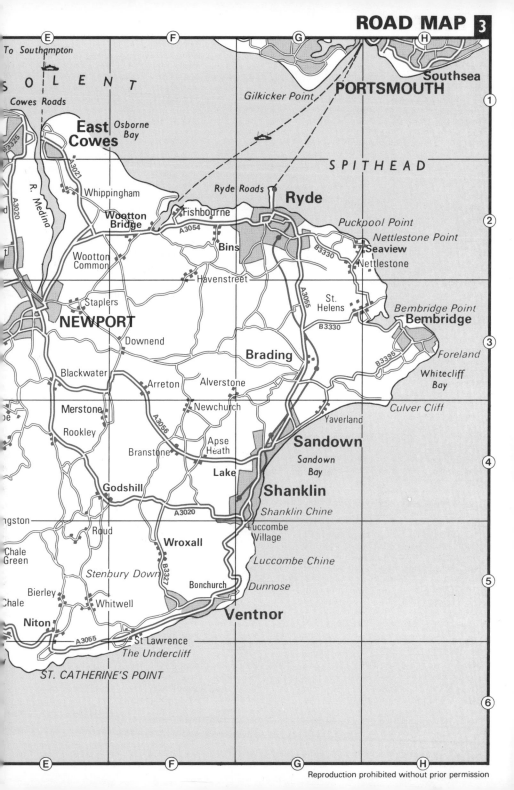

To Southampton

S O L E N T

Cowes Roads

①

Gilkicker Point

PORTSMOUTH   **Southsea**

East Osborne
Cowes Bay

S P I T H E A D

Whippingham

Ryde Roads

Ryde

②

R. Medina

Fishbourne

Wootton
Bridge

A3054

Puckpool Point

Nettlestone Point

Seaview

Bins

B3330

Nettlestone

Wootton
Common

Havenstreet

St.
Helens

Bembridge Point

Bembridge

③

Staplers

NEWPORT

A3055

B3330

B3395

Foreland

Downend

Brading

Whitecliff
Bay

Blackwater

Arreton

Alverstone

Culver Cliff

Merstone

A3056

Newchurch

Yaverland

Rookley

Apse
Heath

Sandown

Branstone

Lake

Sandown
Bay

④

Godshill

A3020

Shanklin

Shanklin Chine

ngston

Roud

Luccombe
Village

Wroxall

B3327

Luccombe Chine

Chale
Green

Stenbury Down

Bonchurch

Dunnose

⑤

Bierley

Whitwell

Chale

Ventnor

Niton

A3055

St Lawrence

The Undercliff

ST. CATHERINE'S POINT

⑥

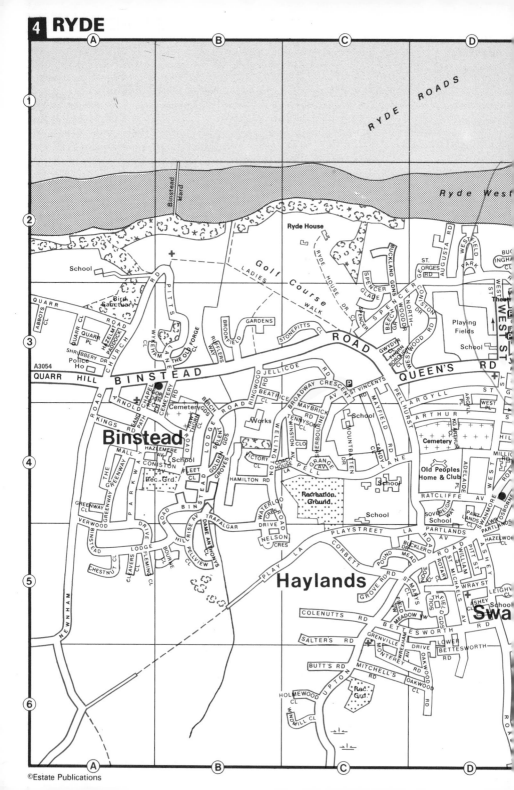

4 RYDE

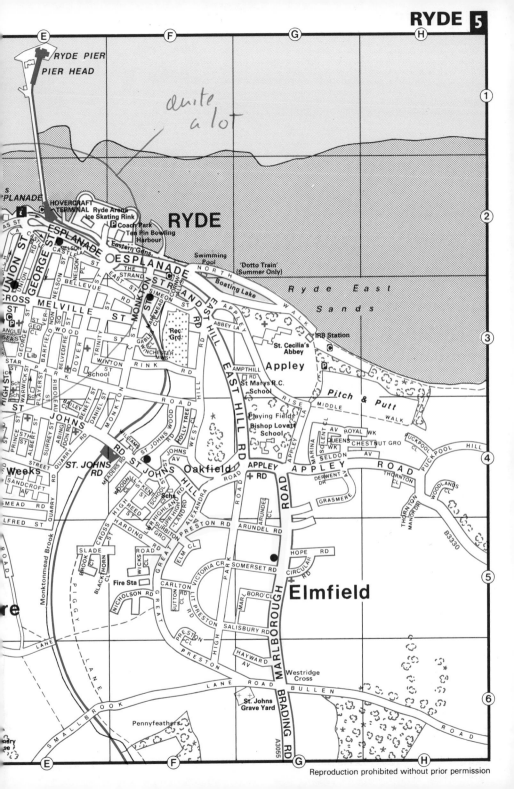

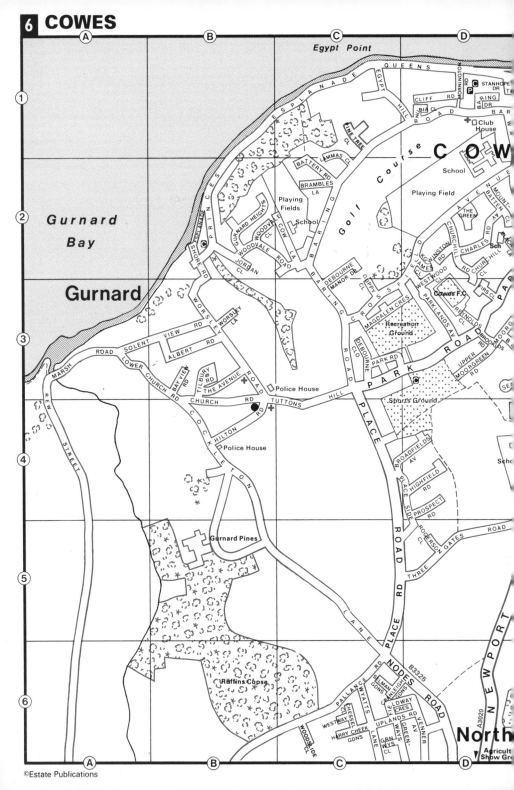

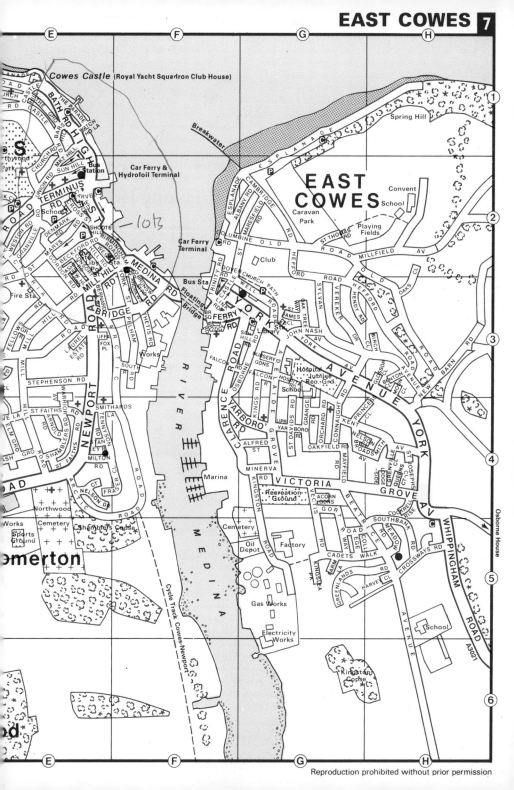

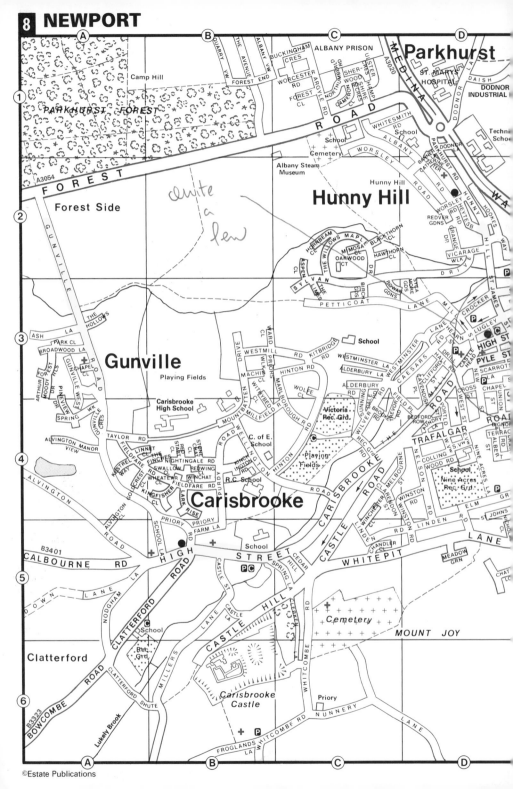

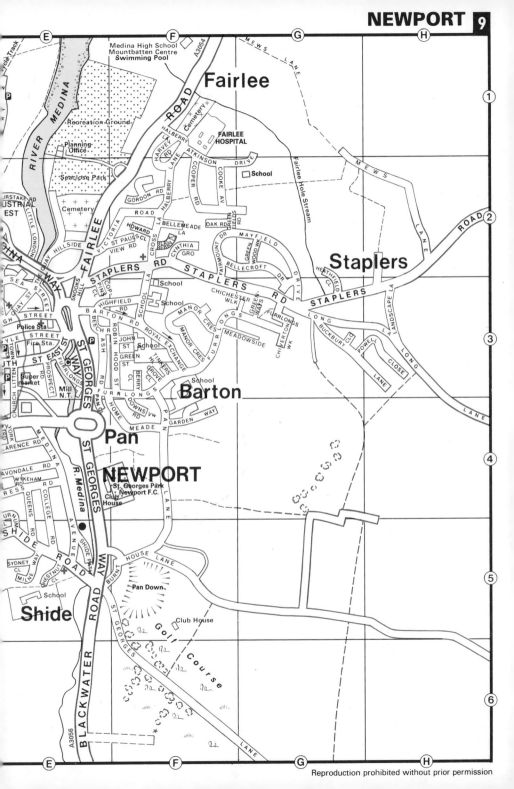

E F G H

Fairlee

Medina High School
Mountbatten Centre
Swimming Pool

A3054

MEWS LANE

Recreation Ground

Cemetery

FAIRLEE
HOSPITAL

Planning
Office

Seaclose Park

Fairlee Hole Stream

□ School

MEWS LANE

Cemetery

RIVER MEDINA

URSTAKE RD
USTRIAL
EST
LITTLE LONDON

HALBERRY LA
HARVEY RD
HALBERRY LA
ATKINSON DRIVE
COOPER RD
COOKE AV

GORDON RD
ROAD

FAIRLEE

VICTORIA ROAD
HOWARD RD
ST PAUL SCL
VIEW RD
CROSS LA
BLACK BERRY
BELLEMEADE LA
OAK RD
GREEN RD
CYNTHIA GRO
FAIRMOUNT DR
GREEN WOOD WK
MAYFIELD

HILLSIDE
SNOOKS HILL
COP PINS
HIGHFIELD RD

Staplers

STAPLERS RD
STAPLERS RD
BELLECROFT DR
CHICHERTON DR
HEATHFIELD CL
STAPLERS

BUCKBURY LANE
LONG LANE
LANDSCAPE LA
POWELL CL
CLOSE
LONG

SEA QUAY ST
STREET
QUAY STREET
Police Sta
STREET
Fire Sta.
PROSPECT
Super
market
Mill
N.T.

BARTON RD
BEECH RD
ROBIN HOOD ST
JOHN ST
GREEN ST
ASH
BERRY
CL
School
ROYAL EXCHANGE
TINKERS
GROVE
DOWNS VW
MANOR CRES
MANOR CRES
FURLONGS
MEADOWSIDE
CHICHESTER WLK
GREEN WAYS
FURLONGS WK

Barton

School

School

School

Pan

ST GEORGES WAY
FURLONGS
PAN CL
HOME CL
MEADE
GARDEN WAY

NEWPORT

St. Georges Park
Newport F.C.
Club
House

R. Medina

CLARENCE RD
AVONDALE RD
WYKEHAM RD
QUEENS RD
COLLEGE RD
MEDINA RD
SHIDE ROAD
URNUM RD
SYDNEY CL
MILNE WAY
CHESTNUT CL

Shide

School

A3056

BLACKWATER ROAD
ST GEORGES WAY
SHIDE PATH
HOUSE LANE
BURNT ST

Pan Down

Club House

Golf Course

LANE

1
2
3
4
5
6

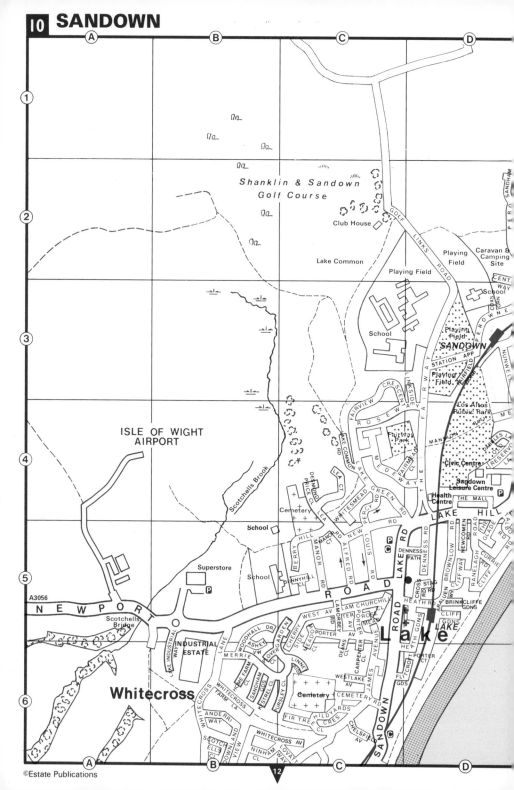

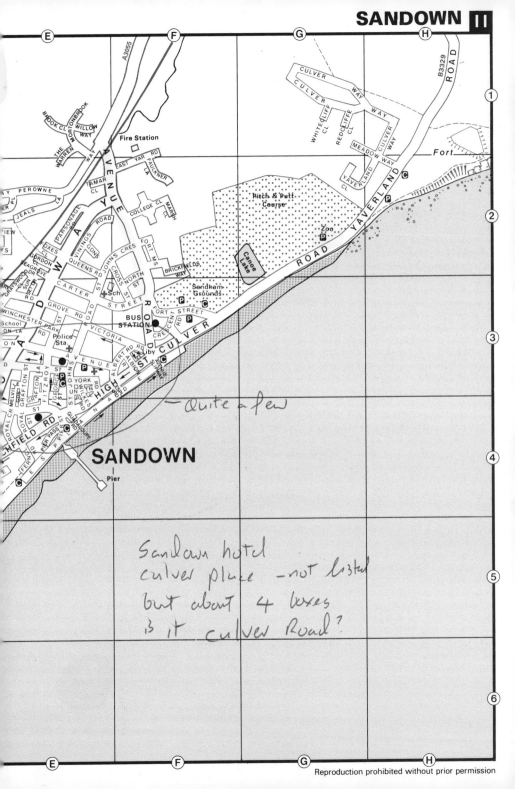

SANDOWN

Pier

—Quite a few

Sandown hotel
culver place —not listed
but about 4 boxes
is it culver Road?

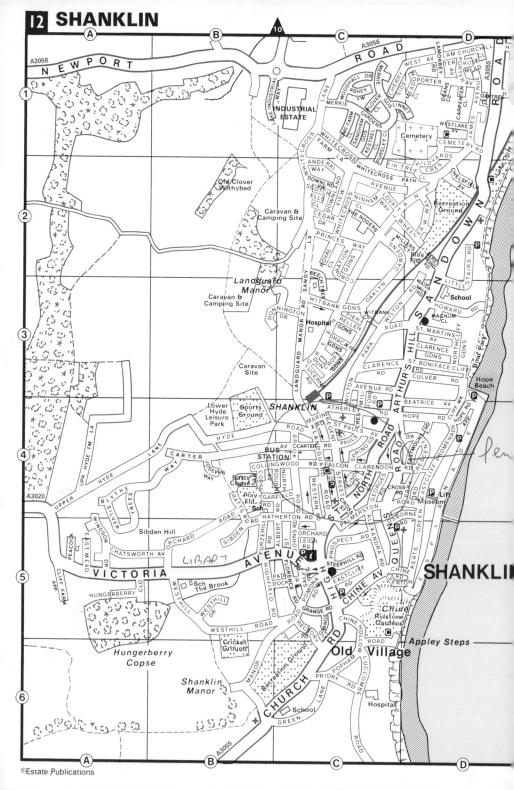

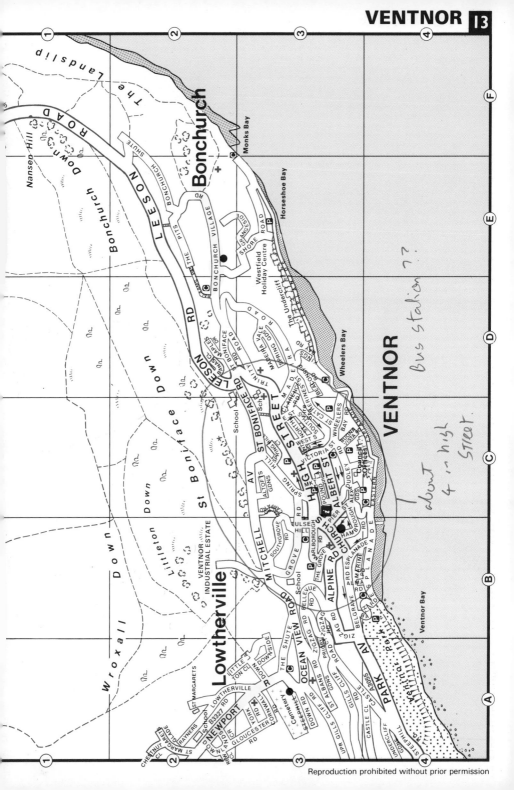

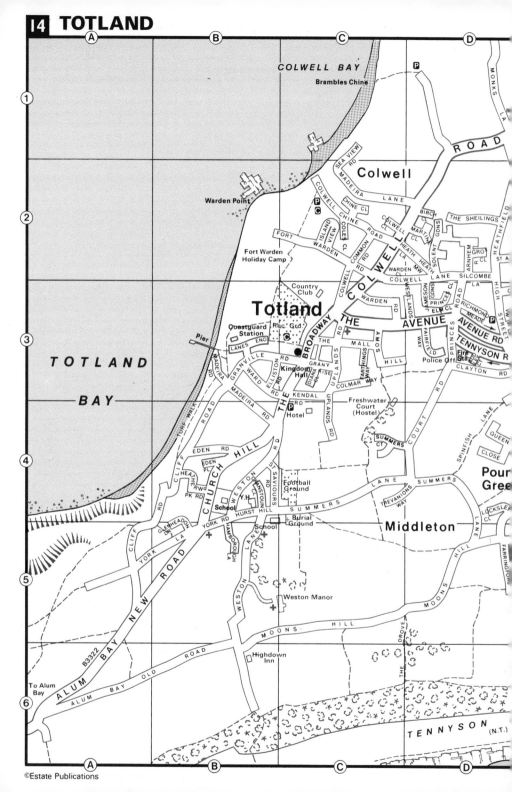

COLWELL BAY

Brambles Chine

Colwell

SEA VIEW RD

MADEIRA LANE

Warden Point

COLWELL CHINE CL

CHINE CL

COLES CL

ISLAND VIEW CL

BIRCH CL

THE SHEILINGS

FORT WARDEN

Fort Warden Holiday Camp

COLWELL CHINE ROAD

COMMON RD

HEATH HEATH

SOLENT GDNS

MARTHA

COLWELL CL

HEATHFIELD

ARNHEM GROVE

CL

STA

Country Club

COLWELL RD

WARDEN CL

WESTLANDS

SILCOMBE

HIGH STREET

Totland

Rec. Grd

THE COLWELL AVENUE

WARDEN RD

J. MESON GDNS

PRINCES RD

RICHMOND MEADE

Coastguard Station

Pier

LANES END

THE BROADWAY

MALL

AMOS

ELM CL

AVENUE RD

P

TOTLAND

MADEIRA ROAD

GRANVILLE RD

WARD RD

Kingdom Hall

GRANV

DIANA RISE

UPLANDS

FARTHINGS WAY

HILL

FAIRFIELD WAY

PRINCES RD

TENNYSON R

Police Off.

Fire Sta.

BAY

ELLISTON RD

ST SAVIOURS RD

COLMAR WAY

CLAYTON RD

KENDAL RD

Hotel

UPLANDS RD

Freshwater Court (Hostel)

COURT RD

SUMMERS CT

SPINFISH LANE

QUEEN

TURF WALK

CLIFF RD

EDEN RD

EDEN PL

HEATHER RD

CHURCH HILL

WESTON RD

Football Ground

LANE

TREVANIONS WAY

SUMMERS WAY

SUMMERS LANE

CLOSE

Pou
Gree

PK RD

School

HURST HILL

Y.H.

St SAVIOURS RD

SUMMERS

Burial Ground

LOCKSLE CL

GLENHEADON DR

YORK LA

YORK RD

HAMBOROUGH RD

School

Middleton

MOONS HILL

FARRINGTON

CLIFF RD

NEW BAY ROAD

WESTON RD

Weston Manor

MOONS HILL

THE DROVE

B3322

To Alum Bay

ALUM BAY OLD ROAD

ALUM BAY

Highdown Inn

TENNYSON (N.T.)

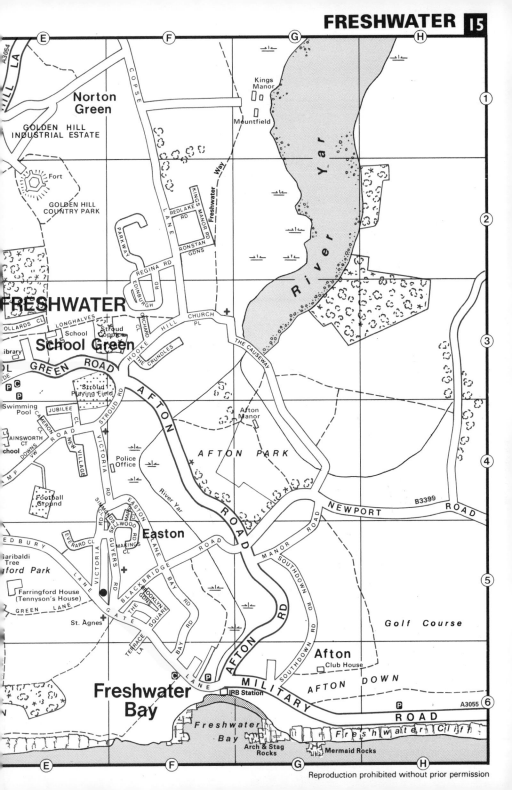

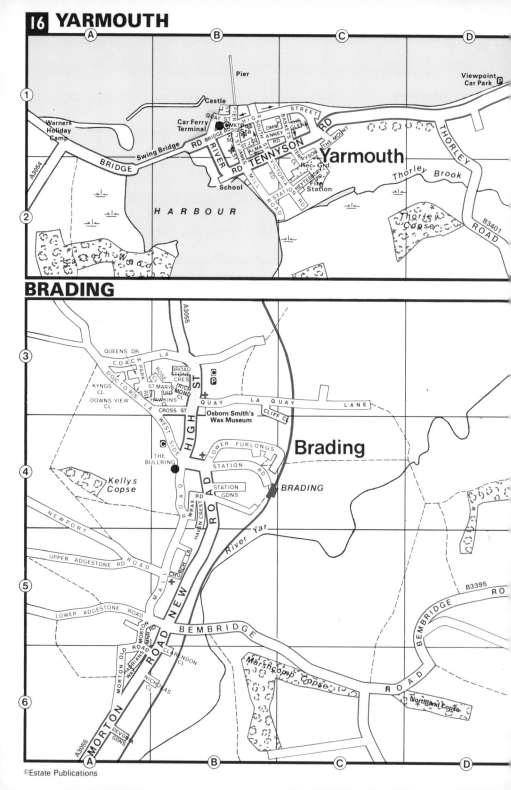

BRADING

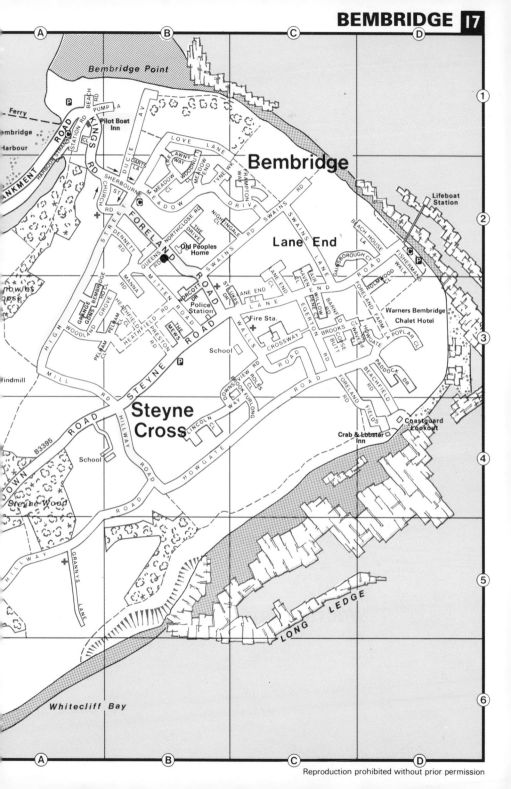

Bembridge Point

Ferry

Bembridge

Harbour

EMBANKMENT

HARBOUR STRAND

KINGS ROAD

STATION RD

Pilot Boat Inn

PUMP LA

BEACH RD

A V

Bembridge

LOVE LANE

TAWNY WAY

WOODNUT CL

MEADOW END

MEADOW

DUCIE

DARTS LA

CHURCH ST

SHERBOURNE RD

FORELAND ROAD

TYNE WK

FRAMPTON WAY

DRIVE

SWAINS RD

NIGHTINGALE CL

THE DRIVE

NORTHCLOSE RD

QUEENS RD

Old Peoples Home

Lane End

SWAINS LANE

GAINSBOROUGH ROAD

Lifeboat Station

BEACH HOUSE LA

FISHERMANS WALK

C P

STREET

DENNETT RD

MANNA RD

HEATHFIELD GROVE

WOODLAND

PELHAM CL

HIGH ST

PELHAM CL

GRANGE GDNS

BEMBRIDGE CL

HEATHFIELD CL

PRESTON RD

THE MEWS

MITTEN ROAD

NORCOTT DR

Police Station

ST LUKES DR

LANE END CL

LANE END CL

LANE END CT

LANE

Fire Sta.

CROSSWAY

WALLS

ROAD

HAVEN RD

AIR PK

PIER LA

EGERTON RD

BROOKS BUTT

CORSE BUTT

BARNFIELD CL

WILLOW CL

WATERS CL

FORELAND FARM LA

HILLGATE CL

POPLAR CL

Warners Bembridge
Chalet Hotel

PADDOCK DR

BEACHFIELD RD

FORELAND RD

FORELAND FIELDS RD

Coastguard Lookout

School

STEYNE ROAD

MILL RD

Windmill

B3395

DOWN ROAD

DOWNSVIEW RD

FOOT FURLONG WAY

ROLLS RD

ROAD

LINCOLN

HOWGATE ROAD

HILLWAY ROAD

Steyne
Cross

School

Steyne Wood

HILLWAY

GRANNYS LANE

Crab & Lobster Inn

LONG LEDGE

Whitecliff Bay

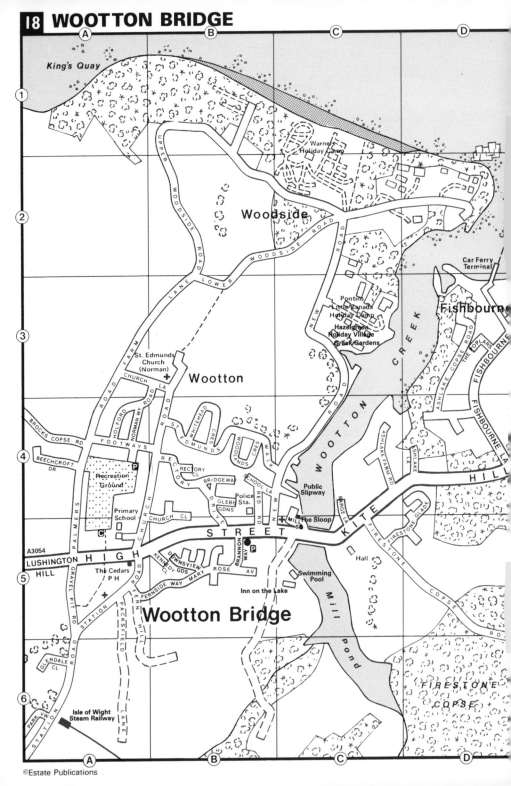

A   B   C   D

1

2

3

4

5

6

King's Quay

Warners Holiday Camp

Woodside

Car Ferry Terminal

Pontins Little Canada Holiday Camp

Hazelgreen Holiday Village Creek Gardens

Fishbourne

St. Edmunds Church (Norman)

Wootton

CREEK

WOOTTON

Recreation Ground

Primary School

Police Sta.

Public Slipway

The Sloop

BEECHCROFT DR

BROCKS COPSE RD

FOOTWAYS

RECTORY CL

BRIDGEWAY

GLEBE GDNS

A3054

LUSHINGTON HILL

HIGH

STREET

The Cedars P H

DOWNSVIEW

KENNEDY GDNS

ROSE AV

MARY

BRANNON WAY

Inn on the Lake

Swimming Pool

Hall

FIRESTONE GLADE

KITE

Wootton Bridge

Mill Pond

Isle of Wight Steam Railway

FIRESTONE COPSE

COPSE RD

FISHBOURNE LA

HILL

ASHLAKE COPSE RD

THE POPLARS

ASHLAKE FARM RD

FIRESTONE

WOODSIDE ROAD

UPPER

LANE

LOWER

WOODSIDE ROAD

NEW

ROAD

ROAD

CHURCH LA

FARM ROAD

HOLFORD

NORMAN WY ROAD

CHURCH

ST EDMUNDS

WHITEHEAD CRES

WOODLANDS CRES

WALK

SCHOOL LA

NEW RD

RECTORY DRIVE

CHURCH CL

PALMERS

GRAVEL PIT RD

STATION ROAD

FERN HILL

PACKSFIELD LANE

GLENDALE CL

PARK TOWN

STATION

FERNSIDE WAY

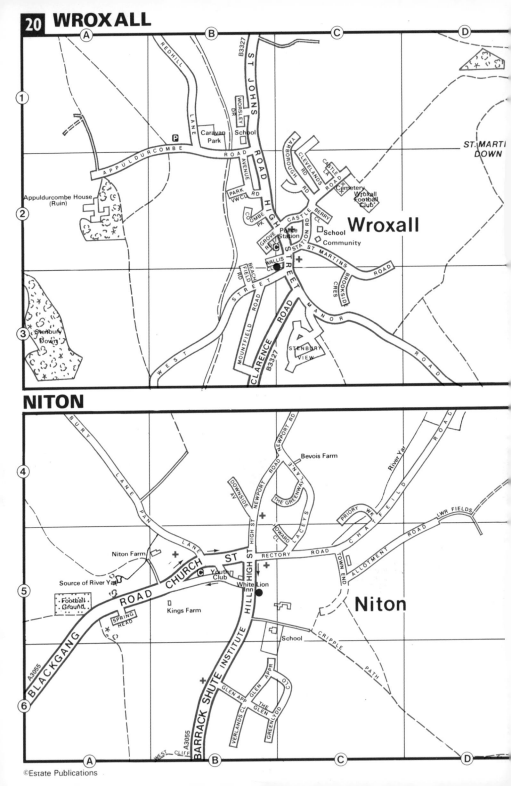

NITON

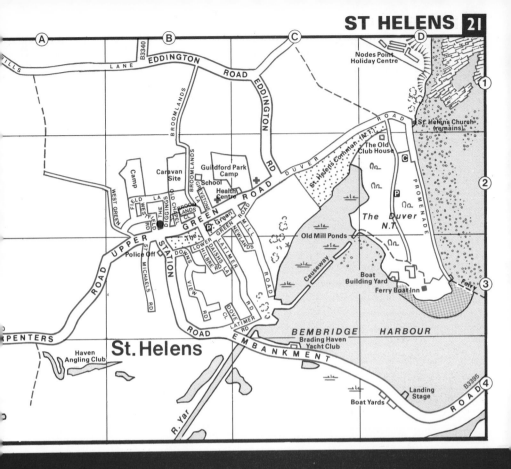

St. Helens

Haven Angling Club

Police Off

Caravan Site

Camp

Guildford Park Camp

School

Health Centre

Old Mill Ponds

The Duver N.T.

Boat Building Yard

Ferry Boat Inn

Nodes Point Holiday Centre

St. Helens Church (remains)

The Old Club House

BEMBRIDGE HARBOUR

Brading Haven Yacht Club

Landing Stage

Boat Yards

R. Yar

A - Z INDEX TO STREETS
with Postcodes

The Index includes some names for which there is insufficient space on the maps. These names are preceded by an * and are followed by the nearest joining thoroughfare.

BEMBRIDGE

...nfield Rd. PO35	17 C3
...ch House La. PO35	17 D2
...ch Rd. PO35	17 A1
...chfield Rd. PO35	17 D3
...035	17 A3
...ok Furlong. PO35	17 C3
...oks Clo. PO35	17 C3
...urch Rd. PO35	17 B2
...pse Butt. PO35	17 C3
...ossway. PO35	17 C3
...arts La. PO35	17 B2
...ennett Rd. PO35	17 C3
...owns View Rd. PO35	17 C3
...ucie Av. PO35	17 B2
...gerton Rd. PO35	17 B2
...rhaven Clo. PO35	17 B2
...shermans Wk. PO35	17 D2
...oreland Farm La. PO35	17 D3

Foreland Flds Rd. PO35	17 C3
Foreland Rd. PO35	17 B2
Frampton Way. PO35	17 C2
Gainsborough Ct. PO35	17 D2
Grange Gdns. PO35	17 A3
Grannys La. PO35	17 A5
Harbour Strand. PO35	17 A1
Heathfield Clo. PO35	17 B3
Heathfield Rd. PO35	17 B3
High St. PO35	17 A3
Hillway Rd. PO35	17 B4
Holmwood Clo. PO35	17 D3
Howgate Clo. PO35	17 D3
Howgate Rd. PO35	17 B4
Kings Clo. PO35	17 A1
Kings Rd. PO35	17 A1
Lane End Clo. PO35	17 C3
Lane End Ct. PO35	17 C3
Lane End Rd. PO35	17 C3
Lincoln Clo. PO35	17 B4
Lincoln Way. PO35	17 B4
Love La. PO35	17 B1
Manna Rd. PO35	17 B3
Meadow Clo. PO35	17 B2
Meadow Dri. PO35	17 B2
Meadow End. PO35	17 B2
Mill Rd. PO35	17 A3
Mitten Rd. PO35	17 B3
Nightingale Clo. PO35	17 C2
Norcott Dri. PO35	17 B3
Northclose Rd. PO35	17 B2
Paddock Dri. PO35	17 D3

Pelham Clo. PO35	17 B3
Poplar Clo. PO35	17 D3
Preston Rd. PO35	17 B3
Pump La. PO35	17 A1
Queens Rd. PO35	17 B2
Rolfs Clo. PO35	17 C3
St Lukes Dri. PO35	17 C3
Sandown Rd. PO35	17 A4
Sherbourne St. PO35	17 B2
Station Rd. PO35	17 A1
Steyne Rd. PO35	17 B3
Swains La. PO35	17 C2
Swains Rd. PO35	17 C2
The Drive. PO35	17 B2
The Mews. PO35	17 B3
Trelawny Way. PO35	17 B2
Tyne Walk. PO35	17 B2
Walls Rd. PO35	17 C3
Wavesound Clo. PO35	17 C3
Willowdene Ct. PO35	17 C3
Woodland Gro. PO35	17 A3
Woodnutt Clo. PO35	17 B2

BRADING

Bembridge Rd. PO36	16 B5
Broadstone Cres. PO36	16 B3
Church La. PO36	16 B5
Clarendon Clo. PO36	16 B6
Cliff Clo. PO36	16 B3

Coach La. PO36	16 A3
Cross St. PO36	16 B3
Devonia Gdns. PO36	16 A6
Doctors La. PO36	16 A3
Downs View Clo. PO36	16 A3
Hadrians Way. PO36	16 A6
Haven Crest. PO36	16 B4
Hawkins Clo. PO36	16 B3
High St. PO36	16 B3
Kyngs Clo. PO36	16 A3
Lower Adgestone Rd. PO36	16 A5
Lower Furlongs. PO36	16 B4
Mall Rd. PO36	16 B5
Morton Manor Rd. PO36	16 A5
Morton Old Rd. PO36	16 A6
Morton Rd. PO36	16 A6
New Rd. PO36	16 B5
Newport Rd. PO36	16 A4
Nicholas Clo. PO36	16 A6
Park Rd. PO36	16 A3
Quay La. PO36	16 B3
Queens Dri. PO36	16 A3
Richmond Clo. PO36	16 B3
Rose Clo. PO36	16 B3
St Marys Rd. PO36	16 B3
Station Gdns. PO36	16 B4
Station Rd. PO36	16 B4
The Bullring. PO36	16 B4
Upper Adgestone Rd. PO36	16 A5

West Side. PO36	16 B4
Wrax Rd. PO36	16 B4

COWES

Acorn Gdns. PO32	7 G4
Adelaide Gro. PO32	7 G3
Albany Rd. PO32	7 F2
Albert Rd. PO31	6 B3
Albert St. PO31	7 E2
Alexandra Rd. PO31	7 E3
Alfred St. PO32	7 G4
Arctic Rd. PO31	7 F3
Arnold Rd. PO31	7 E4
Ash Gro. PO31	7 E4
Ashton Ter. PO31	7 E2
Baring Dri. PO31	6 D1
Baring Rd. PO31	6 C2
Bars Hill. PO31	7 E1
Bath Rd. PO31	7 E1
Battery Rd. PO31	6 C2
Bay View Rd. PO31	6 B3
Beatrice Av. PO32	7 G4
Beckford Rd. PO31	7 E2
Bellevue Rd. PO31	6 D3
Benton Clo. PO32	7 H3
Bernard Rd. PO31	7 E3
Birch Clo. PO32	7 H3
Birmingham Rd. PO31	7 E2
Blackberry La. PO31	6 D2

Brambles La. PO31 6 C2
Bridge Rd, Cowes. PO31 7 E3
Bridge Rd,
E. Cowes. PO32 7 F3
Bridge Sq. PO32 7 F3
Broadfields Av. PO31 6 C4
Broadsmith Av. PO32 7 G4
Brooklands Rd. PO31 6 D3
Brunswick Rd. PO31 7 F3
Cadets Walk. PO32 7 G5
Cambridge Rd. PO32 7 G2
Carvel La. PO31 7 E2
Castle Hill. PO31 7 E1
Castle Rd. PO31 7 E1
Castle St. PO32 7 F3
Charles Rd. PO31 6 D2
Chessel Clo. PO31 6 C6
Church Path. PO32 7 G3
Church Rd. PO31 7 E2
Church Rd,
Gurnard. PO31 6 B3
Churchill Clo. PO31 6 D2
Churchill Rd. PO31 6 D2
Clarence Rd. PO32 7 F4
Cliff Rd. PO31 6 D1
Cockrell Rise. PO32 7 H4
Cockleton La. PO31 6 B4
College Way. PO32 7 G5
Columbine Rd. PO32 7 F2
Connaught Rd. PO32 7 G4
Consort Rd. PO31 7 E2
Coronation Rd. PO31 6 D3
Cow La. PO31 6 C2
Cranleigh Gdns. PO31 6 C6
Cross St. PO31 7 E2
Crossfield Av. PO31 6 C3
Crossways Rd. PO32 7 H5
Debourne Clo. PO31 6 C3
Debourne Manor Dri.
PO31 6 C3
Denmark Rd. PO31 7 E2
Dover Rd. PO32 7 F2
Edinburgh Clo. PO31 6 D2
Egypt Hill. PO31 6 C1
Elm Gro. PO31 7 E4
Esplanade, Cowes. PO31 7 E1
Esplanade,
East Cowes. PO32 7 F2
Esplanade,
Gurnard. PO31 6 B2
Falcon Rd. PO32 7 F3
Farm La. PO32 7 G5
Fellows Rd. PO31 7 E3
Ferry Rd. PO32 7 F3
Fieldway Cres. PO31 6 C6
Firs Clo. PO31 6 D3
Fraser Clo. PO31 7 E4
Glossop Clo. PO32 7 H3
Gordon Rd. PO31 7 E2
Gort Rd. PO32 7 G4
Grange Rd. PO32 7 G4
Granville Rd. PO31 7 E2
Greenlands Rd. PO32 7 G5
Greenways. PO32 6 C6
Greenways Clo. PO31 6 C6
Grenville Clo. PO32 7 H4
Grove Rd. PO31 7 E3
Guppy Clo. PO31 6 C3
Gurnard Heights. PO31 6 B2
Harry Cheek Gdns. PO31 6 C6
Harvey Clo. PO32 7 H5
Hefford Rd. PO32 7 G2
Hendy Rd. PO32 7 G3
High St. PO31 7 E1
Highfield Rd. PO31 6 D4
Hilton Rd. PO31 6 B4
Hospital Rd. PO32 7 G3
John Nash Av. PO32 7 G3
Jordan Clo. PO31 6 B2
Kent Av. PO32 7 G4
King James Clo. PO31 6 D2
Kings Rd. PO32 7 G4
Kingslea Park. PO32 7 G5
Kingston Rd. PO32 7 G4
Lammas Clo. PO31 6 C2
Langley Rd. PO31 7 F2
Laurel Estate Rd. PO31 7 E3
Link Rd. PO32 7 G4
Lodgeside. PO32 7 H4
Love La. PO31 7 E4
Lower Church Rd. PO31 6 A3
Magdalen Cres. PO31 6 C3
Maresfield Rd. PO32 7 G2
Market Hill. PO31 7 E2

Marsh Rd. PO31 6 A3
Maxted Clo. PO31 7 E3
Mayfield Rd. PO32 7 G4
Meadow Rd. PO32 7 H5
Medina Rd. PO31 7 F2
Mill Hill Rd. PO31 7 E3
Millfield Av. PO32 7 G2
Milton Rd. PO31 7 E4
Minerva Rd. PO32 7 G4
Moon Clo. PO31 7 H3
Moorgreen Rd. PO31 6 D3
Mornington Rd. PO31 6 D1
Mountbatten Av. PO31 6 D2
Nelson Clo. PO32 7 G4
Nelson Ct. PO31 7 E4
Nelson Dri. PO31 7 E4
New Barn Rd. PO32 7 H3
Newport Rd. PO31 6 D6
Nodes Rd. PO31 6 C6
Nubia Clo. PO31 6 D1
Nursery Gdns. PO32 7 G3
Oak Tree Way. PO32 7 G3
Oakfield Rd. PO32 7 G4
Oaks Clo. PO32 7 H3
Old Rd. PO32 7 G2
Orchard Rd. PO32 7 G4
Osborne Rd. PO32 7 F3
Pallance Rd. PO31 6 C6
Park Ct. PO31 7 E2
Park Rd. PO31 6 C3
Parklands Av. PO31 6 D3
Pelham Rd. PO31 7 F3
Pine Tree Clo. PO31 6 C1
Place Rd. PO31 6 C4
Place Side. PO31 6 C4
Princes Esplanade. PO31 6 B2
Princes St. PO31 6 D2
Princess Clo. PO32 7 G4
Prospect Rd. PO31 6 D4
Queens Ct. PO32 7 H4
Queens Rd. PO31 6 C1
Rew St. PO31 6 A3
Reynolds Clo. PO31 6 D3
Rogerson Clo. PO31 6 D5
St Andrews St. PO31 7 F3
St Davids Rd. PO31 7 G4
St Faiths Rd. PO31 7 E4
St James Clo. PO32 7 G3
St Josephs Clo. PO32 7 H4
St Marys Rd. PO31 7 E4
St Thomas Rd. PO32 7 G2
School Hill Rd. PO32 7 G3
Sea View Rd. PO31 6 D3
Selman Gdns. PO31 6 C6
Shamblers Rd. PO31 7 E2
Shooters Hill. PO31 7 E2
Shore Rd. PO31 6 B2
Smithards La. PO31 7 E4
Solent View Rd. PO31 6 A3
South Rd. PO31 7 F3
Southbank Rd. PO32 7 H5
Stanhope Dri. PO31 6 D1
Stanley Rd. PO31 7 E4
Stephenson Rd. PO31 7 E3
Sun Hill. PO31 7 E2
Sylvan Av. PO32 7 G3
Tennyson Rd. PO31 7 E4
Terminus Rd. PO31 7 E2
The Avenue. PO31 6 B3
The Cut. PO31 7 E2
The Green. PO31 6 D2
The Grove. PO31 7 E1
The Parade. PO31 7 E1
Thetis Rd. PO31 7 F3
Three Gates Rd. PO31 6 D5
Tilbury Rd. PO31 6 B3
Trinity Church La. PO31 6 D1
Trinity Rd. PO32 7 F2
Tuttons Hill. PO31 6 C4
Uffa Fox Pl. PO31 7 E3
Union Rd. PO31 7 E2
Uplands Rd. PO31 6 C6
Upper Moorgreen Rd.
PO31 6 D3
Upper Yarborough Rd.
PO32 7 G4
Vectis Rd. PO32 7 G4
Venner Av. PO31 6 D6
Vereker Dri. PO32 7 G3
Victoria Gro. PO32 7 G4
Victoria Rd. PO31 7 E2
Ward Av. PO31 6 D1
Warrior Av. PO31 6 D1
Watch House La. PO31 7 E1
Well Rd. PO32 7 G3

West Hill Gro. PO31 7 E3
West Hill Rd. PO31 7 E2
Weston Rd. PO31 7 E2
Westway. PO31 6 C6
Westwood Clo. PO31 6 D3
Whippingham Rd. PO32 7 H5
Windmill Clo. PO31 7 E4
Winston Rd. PO31 6 D2
Woodside Clo. PO31 6 C6
Woodvale Clo. PO31 6 B2
Woodvale Rd. PO31 6 B2
Worsley La. PO31 6 B3
Worsley Rd. PO31 6 B3
Wyatts La. PO31 6 C6
Yarborough Rd. PO32 7 F4
York Av. PO32 7 G3
York St. PO31 7 F2

FRESHWATER

Afton Rd. PO40 15 F3
Ainsworth Ct. PO40 15 E4
Alum Bay New Rd.
PO39 14 A6
Alum Bay Old Rd.
PO39 14 A6
Amos Hill. PO39 14 C3
Arnhem Rd. PO40 14 D2
Audley Ct. PO40 14 D3
Avenue Rd. PO40 14 D3
Bay Rd. PO40 15 F5
Bedbury La. PO40 15 E5
Birch Clo. PO40 14 D2
Blackbridge Rd. PO40 15 F5
Bound Rd. PO40 14 D2
Brooklyn Gdns. PO40 15 E3
Brookside Rd. PO40 15 E3
Cameron Clo. PO40 15 E4
Camp Rd. PO40 15 E4
Chine Clo. PO40 14 C2
Church Hill. PO39 14 B4
Church Pl. PO40 15 F3
Clayton Rd. PO40 14 D3
Cliff Rd. PO39 14 A5
Coles Clo. PO40 14 C2
Collards Clo. PO40 15 E3
Colmar Way. PO39 14 C3
Colwell Chine Rd. PO40 14 C2
Colwell Clo. PO40 14 C2
Colwell Common Rd.
PO39 14 C3
Colwell La. PO40 14 C2
Colwell Rd. PO40 14 C3
Copse La. PO40 15 F1
Court Rd. PO40 14 D4
Cranstoun Clo. PO39 14 B4
Diana Clo. PO39 14 C3
Downs View. PO40 15 E4
Easton La. PO40 15 F4
Eden Pl. PO39 14 B4
Eden Rd. PO39 14 B4
Edinburgh Rd. PO40 15 F3
Elliston Rd. PO39 14 B3
Elm Clo. PO40 14 D3
Everard Clo. PO40 15 E5
Fairfield Way. PO39 14 D3
Farringford Farm Rd.
PO40 14 D5
Farthings Way. PO39 14 C3
Fort Warden Rd. PO39 14 C2
Freshwater Way. PO40 15 F3
Gate La. PO40 15 F5
Glenheadon Dri. PO39 14 B5
Golden Ridge. PO40 14 D3
Goldingsway. PO40 15 E2
Granville Rise. PO39 14 C3
Granville Road. PO39 14 B3
Green La. PO40 15 E5
Groves Clo. PO40 14 D2
Guyers Rd. PO40 15 F5
Hamborough La. PO39 14 B5
Heath La. PO40 14 C2
Heath Meadow. PO40 14 D2
Heatherwood Park Rd.
PO39 14 B4
Heathfield Clo. PO40 14 B4
Heathfield Rd. PO40 14 C2
High St. PO40 14 D3
High View. PO40 14 D3
Hill La. PO40 14 C3
Hooke Hill. PO40 15 F3
Hurst Hill. PO39 14 B4

INDUSTRIAL ESTATES:
Golden Hill Ind Est.
PO40 15 E1
Island View. PO39 14 C2
Jameson Gdns. PO39 14 D3
Jubilee Clo. PG40 15 E4
Kendal Rd. PO39 14 C3
Kings Manor Rd. PO40 15 F2
Lanes End. PO39 14 B3
Locksley Clo. PO40 14 D4
Longhalves. PO40 15 E3
Madeira La. PO40 14 C2
Madeira Rd. PO39 14 C3
Makings Clo. PO40 15 F5
Manor Rd. PO40 15 G5
Marsh Clo. PO40 15 F4
Martine Clo. PO40 14 D2
Military Rd. PO40 15 G6
Monks La. PO40 14 D1
Moons Hill. PO40 14 D3
New Village. PO40 15 E4
Newport Rd. PO40 14 D3
Orchard Clo. PO40 15 F3
Parkway. PO40 15 F2
Princes Clo. PO39 14 D3
Princes Rd. PO40 14 D3
Queens Clo. PO40 14 D4
Queens Rd. PO40 14 D3
Redlake Rd. PO40 15 F2
Regina Rd. PO40 15 F2
Richmond Meade. PO40 14 D3
Ronstan Gdns. PO40 15 F2
St Andrews Way. PO40 14 D2
St Saviours Rd.PO39 14 B4
School Green Rd. PO40 14 D3
Sea View Rd. PO40 14 C1
Sellwood Rd. PO40 15 F5
Silcombe La. PO40 14 D2
Simmonds Clo. PO40 15 F4
Solent Gdns. PO40 14 D2
Southdown Rd. PO40 15 G5
Spinfish La. PO40 14 D4
Stroud Rd. PO40 15 E4
Summers Ct. PO40 14 C4
Summers La. PO39 14 C4
Sunset Clo. PO40 14 D3
Tennyson Rd. PO40 14 D3
Terrace La. PO40 15 F5
The Avenue. PO39 14 C3
The Barbaras. PO40 14 D1
The Broadway. PO39 14 C3
The Causeway. PO40 15 G3
The Crundles. PO40 15 F3
The Drove.PO40 14 C6
The Mall. PO39 14 C3
The Sheilings. PO40 14 D2
The Square. PO40 15 F5
Trevanions Way. PO39 14 C4
Turf Walk. PO39 14 B4
Uplands Rd. PO39 14 C3
Victoria Rd. PO40 15 E5
Ward Rd. PO39 14 B3
Warden Clo. PO40 14 C2
Warden Rd. PO39 14 C3
Westlands. PO39 14 D3
Weston La. PO39 14 B5
Weston Rd. PO39 14 B4
Windmill La. PO40 15 E4
York La. PO39 14 A5
York Rd. PO39 14 B5

NEWPORT

Albany Rd. PO30 8 C1
Albany Vw. PO30 8 B1
Albert St. PO30 8 D4
Alderbury La. PO30 8 C3
Alderbury Rd. PO30 8 C3
Alvington Clo. PO30 8 A5
Alvington Manor Vw.
PO30 8 A4
Alvington Rd. PO30 8 A4
Argyle Rd. PO30 8 C1
Arthur Moody Dri. PO30 8 A3
Ash La. PO30 8 A3
Ash Rd. PO30 9 E3
Aspen Clo. PO30 8 C2
Atkinson Dri. PO30 9 F1
Avondale Rd. PO30 8 D1
Banner La. PO30 9 E3
Barton Rd. PO30 9 E3
Bedford Row. PO30 8 D4
Beech Rd. PO30 9 E3

Bellecroft Dri. PO30 9
Bellemeade La. PO30 9
Berry Clo. PO30 9
Bignor Pl. PO30 8
Birch Gdns. PO30 8
Blackberry Clo. PO30 9
Blackthorn Clo. PO30 8
Blackwater Rd. PO30 9
Bowcombe Rd. PO30 8
Broadwood La. PO30 8
Brooke Rd. PO30 8
Buckbury Clo. PO30 8
Buckbury La. PO30 8
Buckingham Cres. PO30 8
Burnt House La. PO30 9
Caesars Rd. PO30 8
Calbourne Rd. PO30 8
Cameron Clo. PO30 8
Carisbrooke Rd. PO30 8
Castle Hill. PO30 8
Castle Head. PO30 8
Castle La. PO30 8
Castle Rd. PO30 8
Castle St. PO30 8
Catherine Ter. PO30 8
Cavendish Pl. PO30 8
Cedar Hill. PO30 8
Chain La. PO30 8
Chandler Clo. PO30 8
Chapel Clo. PO30 8
Chapel St. PO30 8
Chatfield Lodge. PO30 8
Chestnut Clo. PO30 9
Chichester Walk. PO30 9
Chiverton Walk. PO30 9
Church Litten. PO30 8
Clarence Rd. PO30 9
Clarendon St. PO30 8
Clatterford Rd. PO30 8
Clatterford Shute. PO30 8
Clerken La. PO30 8
Clifford St. PO30 8
College Rd. PO30 8
Collingwood Rd. PO30 8
Cooke Av. PO30 9
Cooper Rd. PO30 9
Coppins Clo. PO30 9
Crocker St. PO30 8
Cross La. PO30 9
Cross St. PO30 8
Cynthia Gro. PO30 9
Cypress Rd. PO30 9
Daish Way. PO30 8
Dodnor La. PO30 8
Down La. PO30 8
Downs View Rd. PO30 8
Drake Rd. PO30 8
Drill Hall Rd. PO30 8
East St. PO30 8
East View. PO30 8
Elm Gro. PO30 8
Fairlee Rd. PO30 8
Fairmount Dri. PO30 8
Field Pl. PO30 8
Fieldfare Rd. PO30 8
Forest Clo. PO30 8
Forest End. PO30 8
Forest Hills. PO30 8
Forest Rd. PO30 8
Froglands La. PO30 8
Furrlongs. PO30 9
Garden Way. PO30 9
Goldcrest Clo. PO30 8
Gordon Rd. PO30 8
Grange Dri. PO30 8
*Grays Wk,
Scarrots La. PO30 8
Green Street. PO30 9
Greenfields Rd. PO30 8
Greenways. PO30 9
Greenwood Walk. PO30 9
Grove Clo. PO30 9
Gunville Cres. PO30 8
Gunville Rd. PO30 8
Gunville West. PO30 8
Halberry La. PO30 9
Hampshire Cres. PO30 8
Harvey Rd. PO30 8
Hawthorn Clo. PO30 8
Hearn St. PO30 8
Heathfield Clo. PO30 9
Heytesbury Rd. PO30 8
High St, Carisbrooke.
PO30 8
High St, Newport. PO30 8

hfield Rd. PO30 9 E3
side. PO30 9 E2
ton Rd. PO30 8 C3
yrood St. PO30 9 E3
me Meade. PO30 9 F4
okes Way. PO30 8 D2
rnbeam Clo. PO30 8 C2
ward Clo. PO30 9 F2
nny Hill. PO30 8 D2
rstake Rd. PO30 9 E2
DUSTRIAL ESTATES:
odnor Ind Est. 8 D1
iver Way Ind Est.
PO30
nn St. PO30 9 F3
strel Way. PO30 8 A4
chington Rd. PO30 8 B4
gfisher Clo. PO30 8 B4
oridge Rd. PO30 8 C3
urnum Clo. PO30 9 E5
dscape La. PO30 9 H3
k Rise. PO30 8 B4
ndry La. PO30 8 D4
den Rd. PO30 8 C5
net Clo. PO30 8 A4
le London. PO30 9 E2
g La. PO30 9 G3
ley St. PO30 8 D3
chin Clo. PO30 8 B3
nners Vw. PO30 8 D1
nor Cres. PO30 9 F3
ple Dri. PO30 8 C2
rlborough Rd. PO30 8 C4
yfield Dri. PO30 9 G2
eadow Green. PO30 8 D5
eadowside. PO30 9 F3
dina Av. PO30 9 E4
dina Way. PO30 8 D1
elbourne St. PO30 8 C4
ews La. PO30 9 H3
ll St. PO30 8 D3
llers La. PO30 8 B6
ilfield Rd. PO30 8 B4
lne Way. PO30 9 E5
mosa Clo. PO30 8 C2
unt Pleasant Rd. PO30 9 F3
ountbatten Dri. PO30 8 D4
lson Rd. PO30 8 D3
w St. PO30 8 D3
ghtingale Rd. PO30 8 B4
ne Acres La. PO30 8 D4
dgham La. PO30 8 A5
rthumberland Rd.
PO30 8 C1
nnery La. PO30 8 C6
ak Rd. PO30 9 F2
akwood Ct. PO30 8 C2
chard St. PO30 9 E3
n Clo. PO30 9 E3
n La. PO30 9 F4
rk Clo. PO30 8 A3
rkhurst Rd. PO30 8 D1
tticoat La. PO30 8 C3
eview Dri. PO30 8A4
rtland St. PO30 8 D4
ors Walk. PO30 9 G3
ry Farm La. PO30 8 B3
ry Rd. PO30 8 B5
spect Rd. PO30 9 E3
e St. PO30 8 D3
rry Vw. PO30 8 B1
y St. PO30 9 E3
ens Rd. PO30 9 E4
reation Ground Rd.
030 8 C4
start Clo. PO30 8 B4
ver Gdns. PO30 8 D2
wing Clo. PO30 8 B4
er Way. PO30 9 E2
oin Hood St. PO30 9 F3
wan Gdns. PO30 8 C3
yal Exchange. PO30 9 F3
Cross La. PO30 8 D3
Georges La. PO30 9 F5
Georges Way. PO30 9 E3
James Sq. PO30 8 D3
James St. PO30 8 D3
Johns Clo. PO30 8 D4
Johns Rd. PO30 8 D5
Nicholas Clo. PO30 9 F2
Pauls View Rd. PO30 9 E3
Thomas St. PO30 8 D3
carrots La. PO30

School La, Barton. PO30 9 F3
School La,
Carisbrooke. PO30 8 B5
Sea St. PO30 9 E3
Sherwood Rd. PO30 8 C1
Shide Path. PO30 9 E5
Shide Rd. PO30 9 E5
Snooks Hill. PO30 9 E3
South St. PO30 9 E3
South Vw. PO30 8 D4
Spring La. PO30 8 C5
Spring Walk. PO30 8 A4
Staplers Rd. PO30 9 E2
Stonechat Clo. PO30 8 B4
Sunningdale Rd. PO30 8 C4
Swallow Clo. PO30 8 B4
Sycamore Gdns. PO30 8 D3
Sydney Clo. PO30 9 E5
Sylvan Dri. PO30 8 C3
Taylor Rd. PO30 8 A4
Terrace Rd. PO30 8 D4
The Avenue. PO30 8 B1
The Finches. PO30 8 B4
The Hollows. PO30 8 A3
The Limes. PO30 8 C3
The Mall. PO30 9 C4
The Quay. PO30 9 E2
The Willows. PO30 8 C2
Tinkers Hill. PO30 9 F3
Town La. PO30 9 E3
Trafalgar Rd. PO30 8 D4
Trevor Rd. PO30 8 C4
Ulster Cres. PO30 8 C1
Union St. PO30 8 D3
Upper St James St.
PO30 8 D3
Vicarage Walk. PO30 8 D2
Victoria Rd. PO30 9 E2
Ward Clo. PO30 8 B3
Watergate Rd. PO30 8 D5
Wellington Rd. PO30 8 B4
West St. PO30 8 D4
West Vw. PO30 8 D4
Westmill Rd. PO30 8 B3
Westminster La. PO30 8 D3
Wheatear Clo. PO30 8 B4
Whitcombe Rd. PO30 8 B6
Whitepit La. PO30 8 C5
Whitesmith Rd. PO30 8 C1
Wilver Rd. PO30 8 C4
Winchat Clo. PO30 8 B4
Winchester Clo. PO30 8 D4
Winston Rd. PO30 8 D4
Withybed Clo. PO30 8 B4
Wolfe Clo. PO30 8 C3
Worcester Rd. PO30 8 C1
Worsley Rd. PO30 8 d2
Wykeham Rd. PO30 9 E4
York Rd. PO30 9 E4

NITON

Allotment Rd. PO38 20 C5
Barrack Shute. PO38 20 B6
Blackgang Rd. PO38 20 A6
Bury La. PO38 20 A4
Chatfield Rd. PO38 20 C5
Church Rd. PO38 20 B5
Cripple Path. PO38 20 C5
Downside Av. PO38 20 B4
Glen App. PO38 20 B6
Greenlydd Clo. PO38 20 B6
High St. PO38 20 B5
Howard Clo. PO38 20 C5
Institute Hill. PO38 20 B6
Laceys La. PO38 20 C5
Lower Fields. PO38 20 D4
Newport Rd. PO38 20 B4
Pan La. PO38 20 C5
Priory Walk. PO38 20 C4
Rectory Rd. PO38 20 B5
Spring Head. PO38 20 A5
The Glen. PO38 20 B6
The Greenway 20 C4
Town Rd. PO38 20 C5
Verlands Clo. PO38 20 B6
West Cliff. PO38 20 B6

RYDE

Abbey La. PO33 5 F3

Abbots Clo. PO33 4 A3
Abingdon Rd. PO33 5 E4
Adelaide Pl. PO33 4 D4
Albert St. PO33 5 E4
Alexandra Rd. PO33 5 F4
Alfred St. PO33 5 E4
Ampthill Rd. PO33 5 G3
Anglesea St. PO33 5 E3
Appley La. PO33 5 G4
Appley Rise. PO33 5 F3
Appley Road. PO33 5 G4
Argyll Pl. PO33 4 D3
Argyll St. PO33 4 D3
Arnold R. PO33 4 A3
Arthur St. PO33 4 D4
Arundel Clo. PO33 5 G5
Arundel Rd. PO33 5 G5
Ashey Clo. PO33 4 D5
Ashey Rd. PO33 4 D5
Augusta Rd. PO33 4 D2
Bailey Clo. PO33 5 E4
Barfield. PO33 5 E3
Beatrice Clo. PO33 4 B3
Beech Gro. PO33 4 C3
Bellevue Rd. PO33 5 E3
Belvedere St. PO33 5 E3
Benett St. PO33 5 E4
Bettesworth Rd. PO33 4 C5
Binstead Lodge Rd. PO33 4 A5
Binstead Rd. PO33 4 A3
Birch Gdns. PO33 4 B4
Blackthorn Clo. PO33 5 E5
Bourne Clo. PO33 4 B5
Brading Rd. PO33 5 G6
Broadway Cres. PO33 4 C3
Brook Clo. PO33 5 E5
Brookfield Gdns. PO33 4 B3
Buckingham Clo. PO33 4 D2
Buckingham Rd. PO33 4 D2
Buckland Gdns. PO33 4 C2
Buckler Dri. PO33 4 D5
Bullen Rd. PO33 5 G6
Butt's Rd. PO33 4 C6
Carlton Rd. PO33 5 F5
Castle St. PO33 5 E2
Cemetery Rd. PO33 4 B4
Chapel Rd. PO33 4 A3
Chestnut Clo. PO33 4 A5
Chestnut Gro. PO33 5 G4
Church La. PO33 5 E3
Church Rd. PO33 4 A3
Circular Rd. PO33 5 G5
Cleavers Clo. PO33 4 A5
Coach House La. PO33 4 B4
Colenutt's Rd. PO33 4 C5
Coniston Av. PO33 4 A4
Coniston Dri. PO33 4 D3
Corbett Rd. PO33 4 C5
Cornwall St. PO33 5 F3
Cross St, Oakfield. PO33 5 E5
Cross St, Ryde. PO33 5 E3
Dame Anthonys Clo.
PO33 4 B5
Daniel St. PO33 5 E4
Derwent Dri. PO33 5 G4
Dover St. PO33 5 E3
East Hill Rd. PO33 5 F3
East St. PO33 5 F2
Edward St. PO33 5 E4
Elm Clo. PO33 5 F5
Esplanade. PO33 5 E2
Field View. PO33 4 C5
Fleet Clo. PO33 4 B4
Fleming Clo. PO33 4 A5
Gables Clo. PO33 5 F3
Garfield Rd. PO33 4 D3
George St. PO33 5 E3
Golden Groves. PO33 4 B4
Gordon Clo. PO33 4 B3
Grange Av. PO33 4 C4
Grasmere Av. PO33 5 G4
Great Preston Rd. PO33 5 F5
Green St. PO33 4 D3
Greenway. PO33 4 A4
Greenway Rd. PO33 4 A4
Grenville Dri. PO33 4 C5
Grove Rd. PO33 4 C5
Gwydyr Clo. PO33 4 C3
Hamilton Rd. PO33 4 B4
Harding Rd. PO33 5 F5
Hawthorn Clo. PO33 4 B4
Hayward Av. PO33 5 G6
Hazelmount Paddock.
PO33 4 A3
Hazelwood Clo. PO33 4 D5

Hazlemere Av. PO33 4 A4
High Park Rd. PO33 5 F6
High St, Oakfield. PO33 5 F4
High St, Ryde. PO33 5 E3
Hill St. PO33 4 D4
Hillrise Av. PO33 4 B5
Holly Tree Clo. PO33 5 F4
Holmewood Clo. PO33 4 C6
Hope Rd. PO33 5 G5
Jellicoe Rd. PO33 4 B3
John St. PO33 4 D3
Kent St. PO33 5 F4
King Arthur Clo. PO33 4 D4
Kings Rd. PO33 4 A4
Ladies Walk. PO33 4 B2
Leighwood Clo. PO33 4 D5
Lind St. PO33 4 D3
Little Preston Rd. PO33 5 F5
Longmead Rd. PO33 5 E4
Lower Bettesworth Rd.
PO33 4 D5
Lower Highland Rd.
PO33 5 F4
Lower Partlands. PO33 4 D5
Marina Av. PO33 5 G4
Market St. PO33 4 D3
Marlborough Clo. PO33 5 G5
Marlborough Rd. PO33 5 G6
Marymead Clo. PO33 5 F3
Maybrick Rd. PO33 4 C4
Mayfield Rd. PO33 4 C3
Meaders Rd. PO33 5 F4
Meadow View. PO33 4 C5
Melville St. PO33 5 E3
Middle Walk. PO33 5 G4
Milligan Rd. PO33 4 D4
Millward Pl. PO33 5 E4
Millward Rd. PO33 4 D4
Mitchell's Rd. PO33 4 C6
Monkton St. PO33 5 F3
Monterey Rd. PO33 4 C6
*Morley Ct,
Brook Clo. PO33 5 E5
Mount St. PO33 4 D4
Mountbatten Dri. PO33 4 C4
Nelson Cres. PO33 4 B5
Nelson La. PO33 5 E2
Nelson Pl. PO33 5 E2
Nelson St. PO33 5 E3
Newnham Rd. PO33 4 A5
Newport St. PO33 4 D3
Nicholson Rd. PO33 5 F5
Node Clo. PO33 4 D5
North Walk. PO33 5 F2
Northwood Dri. PO33 4 C3
Oakwood Clo. PO33 4 D6
Oakwood Rd. PO33 4 D6
Osborne Rd. PO33 4 D4
Park Rd. PO33 5 E3
Parkway. PO33 4 A4
Partlands Av. PO33 4 D5
Partlands Clo. PO33 4 D4
Pell La. PO33 4 C4
Pellhurst Rd. PO33 4 C3
Pellview Clo. PO33 4 B5
Piggy La. PO33 5 E5
Pitt St. PO33 4 D5
Pitts La. PO33 4 B3
Play La. PO33 4 B5
Player St. PO33 5 E3
Playstreet La. PO33 4 C5
Pound Mead. PO33 4 C5
Preston Clo. PO33 5 F5
Prince St. PO33 5 E4
Puckpool Clo. PO33 5 H4
Puckpool Hill. PO33 5 H4
Quarr Clo. PO33 4 A3
Quarr Hill. PO33 4 A3
Quarr Pl. PO33 4 A3
Quarr Rd. PO33 4 A3
Quarry Rd. PO33 5 E4
Queen's Rd. PO33 4 D3
Queens Walk. PO33 5 G4
Ratcliffe Av. PO33 4 D4
Reed St. PO33 5 F4
Riboleau St. PO33 5 E3
Ringwood Rd. PO33 4 B3
Rink Rd. PO33 5 F3
Rosemary La. PO33 4 D6
Rotary Clo. PO33 4 D5
Royal Walk. PO33 5 G4
Rufflers Way. PO33 4 B3
Ryde House Dri. PO33 4 C2
St George's Clo. PO33 5 E3
St George's Rd. PO33 4 D2

St James St. PO33 4 D2
St Johns Av. PO33 5 F4
St Johns Hill. PO33 5 F4
St Johns Rd. PO33 5 E4
St Johns Wood Rd.
PO33 5 F4
St Mary's Clo. PO33 4 C5
St Michael's Av. PO33 4 D5
St Thomas St. PO33 5 E2
St Vincents Rd. PO33 4 C3
Salisbury Rd. PO33 5 F5
Salter's Rd. PO33 4 C5
Sandcroft Av. PO33 5 E4
Sandpath. PO33 4 A4
School St. PO33 5 F4
Seldon Av. PO33 5 G4
Sherbourne Av. PO33 4 C4
Shrubbery Dri. PO33 4 A3
Simeon St. PO33 5 F3
Slade Rd. PO33 5 E5
Smallbrook La. PO33 5 E6
Solent Clo. PO33 5 G4
Solent Gdns. PO33 4 B4
Somerset Rd. PO33 5 G5
South St. PO33 5 E4
Southfield Gdns. PO33 4 D5
Sovereign Way. PO33 4 D5
Spencer Clo. PO33 4 C3
Spencer Glade. PO33 4 C3
Spencer Rd. PO33 4 C3
Star St. PO33 5 E3
Station St. PO33 5 E3
Stonepitts Clo. PO33 4 C3
Sun Pl. PO33 4 D4
Surbiton Gro. PO33 5 F5
Surrey St. PO33 5 E4
Sutton Clo. PO33 5 F5
Swanmore Rd. PO33 4 D4
Tandy Clo. PO33 4 C4
Tennyson Clo. PO33 4 C4
The Mall. PO33 4 A4
The Old Forge Clo. PO33 4 B3
The Strand. PO33 5 F2
Thornborough Clo. PO33 4 C3
Thornton Clo. PO33 5 H4
Thornton Manor Dri.
PO33 5 H4
Trafalgar Rd. PO33 4 B4
Trinity St. PO33 5 E3
Union Rd. PO33 5 E3
Union St. PO33 5 E3
Upper Highland Rd. PO33 5 F4
Upton Rd. PO33 4 C6
Vernon Sq. PO33 5 E3
Verwood Dri. PO33 4 A4
Victoria Cres. PO33 5 F5
Victoria Pl. PO33 4 D3
Victoria St. PO33 4 D3
Victory Clo. PO33 4 B4
Warwick St. PO33 5 E3
Waterloo Cres. PO33 4 B4
Weeks Rd. PO33 4 D4
Well St. PO33 5 E4
Wellington Rd. PO33 4 B4
West Hill Rd. PO33 5 F4
West Pl. PO33 4 D3
West St. PO33 4 D3
Westfield Pk. PO33 4 D2
Westwood Rd. PO33 4 D3
Wicks Clo. PO33 5 F5
William St. PO33 4 D5
Williams Clo. PO33 5 F4
Winchester Mews. PO33 4 B3
Windmill Clo. PO33 4 C6
Winston Av. PO33 4 C4
Winston Clo. PO33 4 C4
Winton St. PO33 5 E3
Wood St. PO33 5 E3
Woodhill Clo. PO33 5 F4
Woodlands Clo. PO33 5 H4
Wray St. PO33 4 D5
Wrexham Av. PO33 4 C6
Wykeham Clo. PO33 4 B3
Yelfs Rd. PO33 5 E2

ST. HELENS

Attrills La. PO33 21 A1
Broomlands. PO33 21 B1
Broomlands Clo. PO33 21 B2
Carpenters Rd. PO33 21 A3
Daishs La. PO33 21 B3
Dove Clo. PO33 21 A3